Squiggle Press

I had a grandfather like Jack's.
He gave me a stool and a little spoon.
I would sit down in his vegetable garden.
He'd cut the top off the apple cucumbers which I'd then get into with my spoon.
I'd tell him all my hopes and dreams and doubts and he listened to every one.
For him, ordinary days were messy and colourful too.
Robyn Dolby, PhD, Secure Beginnings

A beautiful, engaging book for children and any important adult in their lives.
Karen Young, Hey Sigmund

A touching, engaging and thought-provoking story which speaks to not only children and parents, but to all of us. In its apparent simplicity are layers of wisdom: it offers children a language to give words to what would otherwise feel impossible to articulate.
It also gives them a vehicle to course correct us parents who continue on asking the worst question ever!
For parents, it opens our eyes to what we repeatedly fail to see, offering insights and strategies to set up converstions with our children for success.
And perhaps most importantly, it gives value and validation to the ordinarily complex mess of daily life experiences and emotions.

Emil Jackson - Tavistock Clinic, London
Consultant Child & Adolescent Psychotherapist

Belinda Blecher is a child and adolescent psychologist based in Sydney, Australia. She has worked extensively in teaching hospitals, child guidance clinics and early years education settings in both London and Sydney. Belinda also runs her own private psychology practice. She has lectured students, teachers and psychologists on early intervention and promoting mental health in young children throughout Australia.

First published in 2025 by Squiggle Press
2 Hanham Road, Kumeu, Auckland, New Zealand

Printed in China by Asia Pacific Offset.
ISBN 978-0-473-74880-7
A catalogue record for this book is available from the National Library of New Zealand.

For Saba. You bring so much colour to our world. B.B.
For Poppa. L.A.

Not That Question Again?

by Belinda Blecher
& Lisa Allen

What I need most of all is colour, always, always – Claude Monet

Do you love questions? Jack does!
He asks lots of questions, and answers many too.
His mum and dad are always saying,
"Enough with the questions!"

At school, Jack's brain is on fire! It gets bigger every day.
Thanks to his questions, Jack knows many cool facts.
He once asked a question about space and now he knows
that one million Earths can fit inside the sun.
Another time he asked about dinosaurs, and found out they
were the biggest animals ever to have walked on Earth.

But there's one question that has no answer.

And that question is, "How was your day?"

It's the worst question EVER,
because there doesn't seem to be one answer!

It's home time, and Jack's got a surprise for Mum!
Mum gives Jack a big, squeezy hug.
Oooh, that feels so good. Yellow good.

"I've painted you a picture!" he says. "It's big and it's made up of lots of different-coloured squiggles."

"That's really beautiful, Jack," says Mum. "Thank you!"

Mum bundles Jack into the car.
In the rear-view mirror, he sees Mum's lips start to move.
He knows what's coming. Oh, no!
That question!

"How was your day?" she asks.

A grey cloud appears around his head.
It's the same question she asks him after school every day.
He hates it more than boiled broccoli and squishy peas.
More than scratchy scarves or stinky socks.

IT'S THE MOST ANNOYING QUESTION EVER!

“What am I meant to say?” thinks Jack.
“That it was a good day?” But it wasn’t only good.
“That it was a bad day?” But it wasn’t only bad.

Jack can’t put all the colours of his day into words.

“Part of me felt happy.
Part of me felt sad.
Part of me felt angry.
That’s why it’s hard to talk about.”

Jack stares out of the window at the yellow, red, blue, white, silver, black and orange cars whizzing by.
"What are you looking at?" asks Mum.

"I'm looking at my day," says Jack.

Ring! Ring! goes Mum's phone.
"It's Dad!" says Mum.
Jack knows what Dad's going to ask.
That impossible question again!
"How was your day?" asks Dad.
Jack frowns and crosses his arms.
His tummy feels tight and swirly purple.

"Oops, gotta go, video call coming in," says Dad.
"Can't wait to hear about your day later."
Whew. That was close!

Jack scrunches his picture into a ball
and the swirly colours disappear.

Mum stops at the corner shop.
"Here's some money for milk, Jack.
Buy yourself an ice-cream too."

Mack, the shopkeeper, leans over the counter.

"How was your day, Jacky-boy?"

Jack looks down at his feet. He has no words.
All the bright pink excitement he felt is melting away,
like a scoop of ice-cream in the hot sun.

The car slows down and bumps up the driveway. Home at last! Jack brightens up.

He bounces out of the car. But then . . . Oh no! It's Nell, from next door. NOT AGAIN!

Here it comes – the most horrible question ever.
"How was your day today, champ?" says Nell.

“I’m not sure,” says Jack.

He disappears inside, then dashes through the house and into the garden.
Grandpa is watering his plants and smiling at him.

SAME QUESTION ABOUT TO LAUNCH!

“Please don’t ask me how my day was,” says Jack.

“I don’t know the answer!”

Jack slumps on the garden seat and drops his crumpled painting on the ground.

"Steady on there, Jack," says Grandpa. "What's up?"
"Was I meant to feel happy all day?" says Jack, quietly.
Grandpa picks up the painting and smooths it out.

"The answer to how was your day seems to be in your painting."
"But my painting is messy," complains Jack.

"Exactly!" Grandpa replies.
"My day was all sorts of colours."
Grandpa says. "Seeing my friends for coffee was a yellow moment, but getting stuck in traffic was annoying and red. Your painting is messy and colourful, just like a day is meant to be."

Jack thinks hard. "I get it now," he tells Grandpa. "My day was all sorts of colours. Tomorrow, don't ask me how my day was, ask me if I had a colourful day!"

To get the right answer, Jack needs to change the question.

"Did you have a colourful day, Grandpa?" asks Jack.
Grandpa smiles. "I did!"

Jack is surprised. He didn't expect grown-ups to have scribbly, mixed-up, all-sorts-of-colours days too.

The next day is dripping with rain. Jack doesn't mind.
After school, he hurries with Mum to the car.
Jack knows Mum is going to ask that question. Again. And she does!
"How was your day, Jack?"

But Jack has a better question.
"Mum!" he says. "Ask me if I had a colourful day!"
Mum laughs with him. "Of course," she says.
"The more colours in your day, the better your day."

"Then I had the best day," says Jack,
"because it was full of lots of colours!"
He feels orange and warm inside.

"Grandpa! I'm home!" yells Jack.

"And guess who had a very colourful day?"

Children often find the question
"How was your day?"
to be overwhelming because their day may have included so many different feelings and experiences.

Why not ask some of these questions instead:

1. What made you smile today?
2. What did you make that made you feel proud?
3. What did you learn today that you didn't know yesterday?
4. What was your favourite "oops" today?
5. Did anything surprise you today?
6. Did anything make you frown today?
7. Did you do anything brave today?
8. Who were you kind to today?

How I feel.

How I am supposed to feel.